Piano • Vocal • Guitar

WORSHIP
SONGS & STORIES
THE MESSAGE BEHIND THE MUSIC

TEXT BY LINDSAY TERRY

ISBN 978-1-4234-5499-1

HAL•LEONARD®
CORPORATION

7777 W. BLUEMOUND RD. P.O. BOX 13819 MILWAUKEE, WI 53213

Visit Hal Leonard Online at
www.halleonard.com

ABOUT THE AUTHOR

Dr. Lindsay Terry has approximately 35 books and resource manuals to his credit. One of his six books of stories behind famous songs reached #11 on the Christian Booksellers Association's bestseller list across the United States and Canada. He has done extensive research in all categories of Christian music for more than forty years. In addition, he has recorded the stories behind more than 125 favorite songs by personally interviewing the songwriters.

Dr. Terry is a columnist for several national periodicals, including *Singing News*, *Pulpit Helps* and Christianity Today's *Today's Christian*. His song stories appear on several major web sites, including *Christian Broadcasting Network* (The 700 Club) and *Today's Christian Weekly*. He has also written for the *Atlanta Journal-Constitution*, *Tampa Tribune* and the *Dallas Morning News*.

A native of Decatur, Alabama, Terry holds a Bachelor of Arts degree, a Master of Religious Education degree, and a Doctor of Philosophy degree. Two honorary degrees have also been bestowed. He and his wife, Marilyn, an award-winning artist, have three children (Rex, Lance and Amy) and eight grandchildren. They currently live on Anastasia Island, near St. Augustine, Florida.

Nancy and Bill Mull

From: "Nancy and Bill Mull" <nwmull@sbcglobal.net>
To: <musicden@comcast.net>
Sent: Friday, March 13, 2009 2:59 PM
Subject: Hal Leonard Worship Book

I'm looking for a copy of Hal Leonard "Worship Songs and Stories, the Message Behind the Music" with text by Lindsay Terry. It's ISBN 978-1-4234-5499-1, HL00311478, price $14.95. I have one book and need another.

Can you help?

Thanks very much!

Nancy Mull
nwmull@sbcglobal.net

260-925-3942

CONTENTS

BLESSED BE YOUR NAME

Words and Music by Matt Redman and Beth Redman

According to Matt and Beth Redman, "Blessed Be Your Name" was not born out of any one particular circumstance, but out of the events of their whole lives. The Redmans, who live in Brighton, England, were both brought up in difficult circumstances, having a lot of different issues with their fathers. Through the years they have come to realize that worshipping God is a choice, and the best choice they could ever make.

This is the kind of song that Matt and Beth had wanted to write for years. Matt says, "Trust is a beautiful act of worship. It says to God, 'I believe in You—in Your unfailing goodness and greatness—no matter what season of life I find myself in.'"

There are some very tangible things that gave rise to the song. The Redmans were on vacation in the States at the time, and the events of 9/11 were still fresh on the minds of everyone. Matt and Beth became aware of how small our vocabulary seems to be when we try to respond to the dark times of life. Becoming immersed in the spiritual and emotional climate of those days was a key element in writing the song.

Matt said, "Our song is really a song born out of the whole of life—a realization that we all face seasons of pain and unease." Many songs that are meaningful to Christians were born out of human suffering. Someone goes through a dark period in his or her life, and out of the darkness comes a sunbeam—a song! Matt said, "The Psalms are filled with a whole host of intense emotions and expressions toward God. So many of the Psalms were birthed in times of suffering and struggle. The other element that led to the song being birthed at this time was our rereading the book of Job. I think this book is really a book about the sovereignty of God—of which suffering is more a subcategory. At the end of chapter one we read: 'The Lord gave and the Lord has taken away. May the name of the Lord be praised.' Or, as other translations word it, 'Blessed be the name of the Lord.'"

Matt related how people who have heard the song have e-mailed their stories, describing how they've chosen to worship our amazing God, even in the most difficult times of life.

CELEBRATE JESUS

Words and Music by Gary Oliver

In the early 1980s, Gary Oliver, a native Texan and a pianist since age ten, became the music director of Truth Church in Fort Worth, Texas. For several years he wrote a new song each week and taught it to the church congregation. Every Saturday evening he would take his Bible and head for the kitchen, the only large room in their home that had enough space for the studio piano. There in the kitchen, after a brief time of Bible reading and prayer, he would write songs.

In 1988 the church was in a particular phase of ministry when they were trying to do some special things to enhance their work with children. As Easter neared, one of the children's workers approached Gary, telling him that they needed something to help the children understand the meaning of Easter. She explained that they were working on a musical with the children, but all of the songs were slow and sad, and not easily understood by the kids. She said, "We want them to know that even though the cross was very sorrowful, there is joy in the Resurrection and it is okay to celebrate Easter. Would you write a song that we can teach the children?" Gary assured her that he would try to write a suitable song.

He went to his special place in the kitchen and wrote a very simple chorus that he thought would help children to understand that it is wonderful to celebrate the resurrection of Christ, and that we can be joyous because He is alive! We serve the only God who died and then rose again from the dead. He is alive forevermore.

On Easter Sunday, as the children sang their new song, "Celebrate Jesus," something unusual happened. The adult choir joined in with the children, and then the whole place erupted with singing. Gary recalls, "We sang the song for at least forty-five minutes. It interrupted the whole program." It was then that Gary knew the song was unique. "Celebrate Jesus" is now sung in many languages around the world.

DAYS OF ELIJAH
Words and Music by Robin Mark

Robin Mark lives with his wife Jacqueline and their three children in Belfast, a coastal city of his native Northern Ireland. Although he is a successful businessman and a college lecturer at Belfast's Queen University, Robin has another gifting in life—leading worship and writing songs. Invitations come to Mark to minister through music in Europe, America, Canada, Australia, and the Far East.

In 1994, one million people were killed during the Rwandan civil war. It was also the year of the first ceasefire in Ireland. Robin watched an end-of-year review on television and found himself in despair about the condition of the world. He began to question if God was really in control, considering the kind of days they were living in.

He remembers that God answered his questions with, "Yes, I am very much in control, and the days in which you live are special times." Mark sensed that Christians must have integrity and stand for God just as Elijah did against the prophets of Baal.

One Sunday morning in 1995, he remembers coming to the church very early, still thinking about God's answers to him. That morning, during the first of their two services, the pastor spoke from the book of Ezekiel about the valley of dry bones. Mark thought the subject was tremendously meaningful and timely.

During the thirty-minute period between the two services, Mark made his way to the church kitchen where he could be alone, and quickly wrote down the words and chords to "Days of Elijah." Near the end of the second service that morning, he presented the song to the church and they sang it for the very first time as part of their worship.

In answering people who may think the song is a little complex, Mark explains that the Lord told him what to write, and that He has used it in a myriad of ways to help a multitude of people. "Days of Elijah" was launched on a meteor-like flight around the world with the release of the famed CD, *Revival in Belfast*, recorded by Robin Mark and the Christian Fellowship Church in Belfast.

FIRM FOUNDATION

Words and Music by Nancy Gordon and Jamie Harvill

Nancy Gordon, an Alabama native, was already an experienced songwriter, while Jamie Harvill, California-born, only had aspirations to write songs. He had tried his hand at it, but had never been published. The two met in 1988 during a series of services at a small church in Mobile, Alabama. Jamie was the guest song leader and Nancy was playing the piano. During that time, the two decided to make an effort at writing songs together.

Their first opportunity came when they were asked to submit some songs for an upcoming country album. They wrote what they thought was an absolutely fantastic song, "The Belle of the Ball." It was accepted at first, but in the end it was cut from the project. Jamie and Nancy were both disappointed—big time. Jamie said, "We found that the saying is true: 'It's not final till it's on the vinyl.'"

Later, during a phone conversation, Nancy said to Jamie, "Just this morning I saw a phrase in the Living Bible, 'I have a living hope.' When I read that, a deep desire welled up within me to sing those words." Jamie replied, "We were wrong to put so much hope in men. We need to pick up and go forward." Nancy said, "We have a living hope!" Jamie answered, "And we have a future." They were aware that they had placed their hope in a song they had written instead of the Lord.

Nancy and Jamie literally talked themselves into the song "Firm Foundation." They were exhorting one another to not be discouraged and to put their hope in God's Holy Word. Most of the lyrics were written over the phone. During the weeks that followed, they got together a couple of times to tweak the song. Jamie's wife commented, "Well, country music didn't get a good song, but the church got a great one!" Integrity Music included the song on an album called *Firm Foundation*, and it is now sung in thousands of churches around the world.

FOREVER

Words and Music by Chris Tomlin

In a recent *TIME Magazine* article, Belinda Luscombe says of Chris Tomlin, "According to CCLI, Tomlin, 34, is the most often sung contemporary artist in U.S. congregations every week… That might make him the most often sung artist (songwriter) anywhere."

While still a student at Texas A&M University, Tomlin began writing "Forever." He said, "I wrote most of the lyrics, but I couldn't finish it. It seemed to take forever to write "Forever."

In Psalm 136, the phrase "for His mercy endureth forever" appears at the close of each verse. Chris could imagine the Israelites quoting that phrase in unison as the Scriptures were being read. He wanted to create something of that same approach with this song—to sing a line and have people respond with "His love endures forever." He wanted desperately to complete the song, and was encouraged by people who heard parts of it, but for four long years he found it difficult to finalize.

At a summer camp where he was leading worship, he decided to work on the song one afternoon during free time. He sang "Forever God is faithful" repeatedly. He wanted to follow that line with the same phrase, but replace the last word. He worked for several afternoons, but could not find the word that he thought would be an appropriate ending for the phrase.

Janet Reeves, the wife of the bass guitarist in his band, was in the room across the hall one afternoon and heard Chris struggling with his songwriting task. She heard him repeatedly get to the same place and stop. She knocked on his door, and as he opened it she said, "The word is *strong*." Chris thought, "That's it! That's the word I need to finish my song."

Chris began to use the song in concerts and worship services with a great response from the audiences. He said, "A year later someone handed me a copy of one of Michael W. Smith's *Worship* albums. 'Forever' was the lead song on the project. I had no idea that he had recorded it. That greatly helped 'Forever' to be known across the nation."

GIVE THANKS

Words and Music by Henry Smith

Henry Smith's songwriting ventures started very early in his life. One day while still in his teens, Smith picked up his brother's guitar (ordered from a Sears catalog) and learned how to play it by reading the instruction manual. Along with his playing came the urge to write songs. His passion for songwriting has lasted to this day. Of the nearly 300 songs he has written, only one has been published. That's right, only one—but what a song!

In 1972, while Smith was a sophomore at King College in Bristol, Tennessee, the Lord seemed to increase His blessings as He poured out His Spirit upon Henry. In response, he began setting the Psalms to music, which revitalized his songwriting. A few years later, while attending the Williamsburg New Testament Church in Virginia, he heard the pastor teach from the Scriptures about how Jesus became poor in order that we might be made rich in Him. Later, in his apartment, he wrote the song "Give Thanks." Not long thereafter, Henry and his future wife, Cindy, sang it at the church. Over a period of several weeks they repeated it a number of times.

A military couple who attended the church during those weeks learned the song and carried it back to Germany where they were stationed. Smith recalls, "As far as I know, that is how my song got to Europe. It did a lot of traveling before Integrity Music published it. It is a 'God thing' that it took off as it did." To date, more than fifty companies have recorded "Give Thanks," and it has been published in a number of songbooks and hymnals. It has become one of the most widely-used songs by churches in the United States.

Several years after the song was written, Henry and Cindy attended a live Integrity Music recording session in Washington, D.C. During the session, Don Moen played a recording that featured Henry's song being sung in Russian. Henry recalls, "My wife and I began to weep. We were overwhelmed to hear my song sung in that language. Moen had no idea we were in the audience."

GOD OF WONDERS

Words and Music by Marc Byrd and Steve Hindalong

A "wake up call" was transmitted to Rick Husband, Commander of the Space Shuttle Columbia, as it orbited planet Earth: "Good morning! That song was for Rick. It was 'God of Wonders' by Steve Green." Rick answered back, "Good morning! Thank you! We can really appreciate the lyrics of that song up here. We look out the window and see that God truly is a God of wonders!"

A few days later, President Bush had the solemn task of announcing to the world that Columbia did not return safely to Earth. The spacecraft had disintegrated during re-entry and fallen in bits and pieces in the southern part of the United States.

Marc Byrd is a self-taught musician who started playing guitar at age thirteen. After his college days, and following several years of touring with a Christian band called Common Children, Marc came to a crossroads in his life. He said, "I didn't know what the future held for me, or even where the next penny was coming from." The one thing Marc did know was that he needed to rely on the Word of God. So, he grabbed his Bible and his guitar one Friday in 1999, and spent the weekend reading the Psalms and rededicating his life to the Lord. The beginning of "God of Wonders" came out of the Psalms during that weekend. He had the music and a few lyric phrases, one of which was "You are holy."

Marc took the music for "God of Wonders" to Steve Hindalong, a dear friend with whom he had written a number of songs. Steve said, "As Marc strummed the chord progression, the hair stood up on my arms. It gave me a chill. It just felt really vast to me. I told Marc, 'This song sounds to me as if it should be like, *God of wonders, beyond all galaxies.*'"

It took them several days, working together, to finish the song. Steve was the primary lyricist and Marc mainly wrote the music. Since then, scores of artists have recorded it, one of whom was Steve Green. It has spread around the world and has been translated into several languages.

While talking with Marc, as he was reflecting on the events connected with the Space Shuttle Columbia, he remarked, "We heard about the playing of our song in space and thought, 'Whoa! That's really cool!'" To which I replied, "That's more than cool, son. That is awesome! That beats cool all to pieces." Marc laughed and readily agreed.

GOD WILL MAKE A WAY

Words and Music by Don Moen

A tragedy in Don Moen's family was the background for one of his most influential and widely-known songs. Moen, currently the President of Integrity Music, related to me the heartbreaking event which led to the writing of "God Will Make a Way."

Don's sister-in-law, Susan Phelps, her husband Craig, and their four children were involved in a serious car accident during a ski trip from their Oklahoma home to a resort in Colorado. At a remote intersection in the Texas panhandle, their van was struck by an eighteen wheeler. The children had just left their seats, where they had been buckled in, to lie down for a nap on a "bed" positioned in the rear of the van. The van was hit with such force that all four of the Phelps' children were thrown out.

In the darkness, they were able to locate their injured children by their crying—all except their nine-year-old son, Jeremy. Craig, who was a medical doctor, finally found him lying beside a nearby fence. He had died upon impact when his neck was broken. As Craig picked up his son and tried to revive him, he felt as if God said to him, "Jeremy is with me. You deal with those who are living." They sat for forty-five minutes out in the wilderness, waiting for an ambulance.

Don was asked to sing at Jeremy's funeral. While traveling by plane to Oklahoma, he began to read in Isaiah chapter 43 where God says, "I will even make a way in the wilderness and rivers in the desert." He picked up his legal pad and sketched a song that the Lord was giving him. He planned to sing it at the memorial service. When he arrived, he learned that the Phelps had already selected Henry Smith's song, "Give Thanks," for him to sing.

After the funeral, Don held Susan and Craig in his arms and said, "The Lord gave me a song for you." He began to sing, "God will make a way, where there seems to be no way." He later made a taped copy of the song for Susan to play on her small cassette player just above her kitchen sink. He knew that when all of the people had gone, and everything was said and done, there would be days when she needed to hear that God was working in ways that she couldn't see.

God does work in many ways that we do not understand. After hearing that Jeremy had become a Christian before the accident, many of his friends began asking how they might know Christ, so that they could also go to heaven when they died.

GREAT IS THE LORD

Words and Music by Michael W. Smith and Deborah D. Smith

While visiting a record company in Nashville, Tennessee, Michael W. Smith saw Debbie Davis walk by. It was love at first sight. He quickly called his mother and said, "Mom, I just saw the girl I am going to marry!" "Really? Who is she?" his mother asked. His excited reply was, "I don't know. I'll have to call you back." He learned her name from others in the building, and went looking for her. He finally spotted her coming out of the ladies' room, and quickly introduced himself.

Little did Debbie realize that she would soon be the wife of this man, who would later become one of the most notable singers and songwriters in the world of Christian music, and that millions of people would sing the songs they would write together. They were married about five months after that chance meeting.

Debbie enjoyed being around the keyboard with Michael. Sometimes at night, by candlelight, they would open the Bible and allow God to speak to them through His Word. They wrote worship songs during those sessions. In 1982, they found a Scripture that they thought would be the background for a wonderful song. While Michael was working on the music, Debbie wrote some words that she hoped would fit what Michael was composing. The words and the musical setting of "Great Is the Lord" came together perfectly.

Michael often led worship at their church, so he taught the song to the congregation. Everyone seemed to move into a spirit of worship as they sang "Great Is the Lord." Debbie said, "I remember I was so overwhelmed as I heard that great crowd lifting their voices in praise as they sang our song. The massiveness of the people around me sounded like a large choir. I felt so blessed to be used in that way."

During those days, Michael was working on his first album, *The Michael W. Smith Project*, and he decided to include "Great Is the Lord." The song continues, year after year, to be a popular worship song in churches across America.

HE IS EXALTED

Words and Music by Twila Paris

Twila Paris was taught to play the piano by her dad, evangelist Oren Paris. She became a songwriter at the age of seventeen. Of the many songs she has written she said, "My songs are like children who will grow and expand and do things I could never do. They make their way around the world as they are being used for the purpose God gave them. 'He Is Exalted' has gone far beyond the people who know my name."

As was her custom, she was sitting at the piano in her parents' home one day, quietly worshipping the Lord. During those times, she would usually sing one of her songs, or another song that was particularly meaningful at the moment. On this very notable day, "He Is Exalted" was given to her by the Heavenly Father. She recognized the moment and knew that this gift from the Lord was something extra special. She said, "It was like taking dictation."

Twila first sang "He Is Exalted" during a Sunday service at the YWAM (Youth With A Mission) base in Arkansas, where she was the worship leader. This was her "test" for the song. A short time later she was surprised and delighted to learn that people in churches across America knew her song. It just seemed to make its way from town to town. There was never a big introduction or splash. It was a gradual thing.

While watching a network television news show one day, she saw a report that seemed to be of a Christian nature. During some comments, the producers of the program cut away to a congregation singing "He Is Exalted." Twila said, "For several moments it was almost surreal. It took me a few seconds to realize, 'Hey, that's my song.'" She then added, "I hope I never get used to hearing my songs."

Paris has written approximately 200 songs, many of which have been recorded or published. When she considers the ministry of songwriting the Lord has graciously given, she thinks of the impact the songs have had on the world—and she is grateful.

THE HEART OF WORSHIP

Words and Music by Matt Redman

Several years ago in England, in the church where Matt Redman was the worship leader, it became apparent that the worship times during their services had become strained—they had somehow lost the meaning of real worship. The "fire" they had experienced in the past seemed to have faded.

Everything looked great on the surface. The church was blessed with talented musicians, quality equipment and a variety of new songs to sing. But they had begun to rely on those things to help them have the kind of worship service they desired. Those "things" had actually become distractions. In fact, some people did not really enter into worship unless they liked the talent of the singers, the quality of the sound, the choice of songs, and whether the singers were really "into" the music.

Pastor Mike Pilavachi took a surprising course of action. One Sunday, as people entered the church, there was no sound system and no band to lead the worship time. Mike had decided that they should not lean on "outward" things if their worship was to be true and sincerely from the heart. He would say, "When you come through the doors of the church on Sunday, what are you bringing as your offering to God? What are you going to sacrifice today?" He may have had Jeremiah 33:11 in mind, which instructs us to "bring the sacrifice of praise into the house of the Lord."

By his own admission, Matt was rather offended by the whole situation. After all, worship was his job! Although the services were awkward at first, Matt soon recognized the pastor's wisdom. People began to offer their sincere and true praise to the Lord without the "trappings" they had gotten used to.

After several weeks, the sound system and the worship band returned to their places, but now with a different attitude and a renewed sense of true worship. Out of this experience, Matt wrote "The Heart of Worship." This song brings us to a recognition of the majesty and deity of Christ, and encourages us to discover the real heart of worship: "It's all about You, Jesus."

HOLY IS THE LORD

Words and Music by Chris Tomlin and Louie Giglio

Louie Giglio is founder and director of the Passion conferences for college-age students, and Chris Tomlin is one of the major worship leaders. Both were instrumental in the writing of "Holy Is the Lord." In 1997, while flying from Waco, Texas to Atlanta, Georgia, the Lord spoke to Giglio's heart about starting a national ministry to students. Thousands of young people now flock to his Passion conferences each year. Chris gave me the story behind "Holy Is the Lord" during a 2005 interview.

Chris was reading Isaiah chapter 6 during his devotional time. After reading verse 3, "Holy, holy, holy is the LORD of hosts. The whole earth is full of his glory," he picked up his guitar and began to sing those words. He was preparing to lead worship at an upcoming Passion conference, which was to be held on a large ranch outside of Dallas, Texas. He sensed that God wanted him to use the song he was writing at the conference, though it was still incomplete.

Chris went to Louie and said, "I have this song, 'Holy Is the Lord,' and I feel that it is for the upcoming Passion conference." He then sang the song for him. Louie began to give Chris a number of ideas that were in his heart. Among other things he helped with the phrase, "It's rising up all around; it's the anthem of the Lord's renown."

Chris took Louie's suggestions and ran with them. He said, "Although I felt that the song was from the Lord and should be used in the meeting, at that time I had never played the song completely through. I arrived at the Passion conference and found that I was to lead worship following a preacher named John Piper, a gifted communicator and writer. While he was on the stage speaking, I was behind the platform on my knees in the grass. I was praying, 'Lord, I want to lead these people in the right way, with the right songs. You just show me what to do.'

"John Piper started his message by saying, 'Students, God has put a message for you on my heart. It is from Isaiah chapter 6—Holy, holy, holy is the LORD of hosts. The whole earth is full of his glory.' That floored me, right there in the grass. I thought, 'God put a song in my heart two months ago. He knows I will follow John Piper and He puts the same message on both our hearts.' At that moment it was confirmed in my heart that I was to use that song."

I SING PRAISES

Words and Music by Terry MacAlmon

Terry MacAlmon's most famous song, "I Sing Praises," is sung in many countries—the United States, England, Canada, Mexico, China, Russia, Argentina and the Philippines, to name a few. Its popularity seems to be still on the rise.

Terry became the Worship Pastor of Resurrection Fellowship Church in Loveland, Colorado in 1986. As was their custom, the ministry leaders of the church would meet for prayer thirty minutes before each service. One Sunday evening during this prayer time, Terry was quietly worshipping the Lord, almost oblivious to others in the room. Suddenly the Lord spoke to his heart, and the result was the creation of a new worship song. Terry said, "It was as if the Lord went over to the music library of heaven and took something out of the 'I' file and dropped it right into my heart." He took a piece of paper from his Bible and jotted down the lyrics and melody line as they were coming to him. He then tucked the paper back into his Bible.

As he led the music portion of the service that evening, he sensed the Holy Spirit prompting him to teach his new song to the congregation. His silent response was, "THAT song? There's nothing to that song. It has no substance and it's too simple." He wondered if Satan might be trying to persuade him not to share what the Lord had given him. Terry sat and stared at the piano keys for what seemed an eternity, trying to decide—to sing it, or not to sing it. There were about 2,000 people awaiting his decision. They didn't know what was taking place in his mind.

Finally he said, "Folks, I would like to teach you a song that the Lord gave to me just before the service tonight." As he started to sing, a weight lifted from his heart. He was amazed at the congregation's response. They picked it up quickly and began to sing along. That night the congregation joyfully sang "I Sing Praises" again and again. Two years later, Terry submitted the song to Integrity Music and it was included on an album entitled *Enter His Gates*.

I STAND IN AWE

Words and Music by Mark Altrogge

Mark Altrogge became excited about the Beatles at age fourteen. He was not a Christian at the time, so all he wanted to do in life was play guitar, get into a band, and be just like them. It was not until ten years later, through the influence of his parents, that his interests were turned toward spiritual matters.

During a Bible study in 1974, with genuine repentance as the subject, Mark discovered what it meant to wholeheartedly surrender his life to the Lord. He soon realized that he would have to give up the rock and roll band that he had formed. He said, "We were playing in places and using music that I knew was not God-glorifying, so I quit the band and began to follow the Lord."

Mark wrote his popular worship song "I Stand in Awe" in 1988, while serving as worship leader for Lord of Life Church in Indiana, Pennsylvania. He had been studying the attributes of God. Several books were influential in his life at the time, including *The Holiness of God* by R.C. Sproul, *The Knowledge of the Holy* by A.W. Tozer, and particularly *The Attributes of God* by Stephen Charnock. The writings of Charles H. Spurgeon were also very meaningful.

Mark said, "I began to reflect on the beautiful truth that God is infinite in each of His attributes; in His beauty, His holiness and His wisdom. He is unsearchable! We will never come to an end of learning new things about Him—even throughout eternity." During those days he tried to write a song capturing the thoughts of his heart. The first phrase came quickly—acclaiming the beauty of God and the marvel of His being. Then came our response to His beauty—a feeling of awe. Mark had an idea for the chorus, but it took several days to work out the completion of the song.

Mark admits that, in all of his songwriting, he has only written one song completely in one sitting. He says, "For me, writing a song is much like preparing a sermon. I do a lot of writing and rewriting. There is some trial and error. It took a good amount of labor to get 'I Stand in Awe' to a state of completion. I am grateful for the assistance of two friends, Bob Cauflin and Steve Cook, who made suggestions, strengthening the song."

From Lord of Life Church, where Mark first sang "I Stand in Awe," it has made its way around the world. Mark has written more than 400 songs, with around 150 of them recorded or published.

I Worship You, Almighty God

Words and Music by Sondra Corbett-Wood

Sondra Corbett-Wood began her songwriting career during her student days at Christ for the Nations Institute in Dallas, Texas. She was influenced in those efforts by two fellow students: Marty Nystrom, author of "As the Deer," and Tommy Walker, who wrote "He Knows My Name."

Sondra was part of a singing group that went out to represent the school and to minister in local churches. One Saturday morning, she went to the music building to worship and pray for the church where her group would sing the following morning. She entered one of the rooms and began to pray for the group's preparation and for the people who would attend. She said, "I had no intention of writing a song."

There was a piano in the room, so she began to play and sing songs to the Lord. She felt a strong sense of God's presence as she sang. Unexpectedly, out of her mouth came, "I worship You, Almighty God; there is none like You." Following that line was another. She immediately thought, "I'm getting a song here!" She ran to the office and asked someone for a pencil and paper, and then hurriedly jotted down the words and the chords to the song.

Sondra explains, "The song came directly from prayer and a desire to commune with the Lord. It was my response. God is the focus of the song." She gave the song to one of the worship leaders at the school, who taught it to the students at a chapel service. They learned it quickly and sang it joyfully.

After graduating from CFNI, she returned to her Kentucky hometown of 175 people. Her mailbox began to fill up almost daily with requests to use her song, which had been recorded by Word Music. A friend told Sondra that her song was listed on the cassette tape as "Author Unknown." Sondra phoned Word and politely stated that she was the author of the song. The Word representative said, "Ma'am, just because you say you wrote a song doesn't mean we are going to send you a check!" Sondra said, "What do you mean, a check?" She thought to herself, "Is money involved?" She hadn't thought of that—she was only excited that her song was being used. Shortly after that phone conversation she received her first royalty check in the mail. She said, "I was amazed at God."

JESUS, NAME ABOVE ALL NAMES

Words and Music by Naida Hearn

Naida Hearn never dreamed that she would influence Christian singing around the world, but she has done just that. In 1974, in Palmerston North, New Zealand, she wrote her only published song, although she has written about twelve others.

As Naida was studying the Bible, she became fascinated by the different names referring to Jesus. So great was her interest that she made a list of the names, and she found great pleasure in reviewing them and thinking about what they meant. Typical of many homes in that area, she and her family had a washhouse behind their regular living quarters. One day she carried her list of the names of Jesus to the washhouse. She placed the list on the windowsill and let it lean against the window, where it was in full view as she did the family washing.

That day she was in a very worshipful mood and began to sing. She said, "The Lord just gave me the first line and I sang, 'Jesus, name above all names.' I just started it and carried on singing. I sang the whole song just as you sing it today. I just opened my mouth and all of the words came out, the pitch and everything. I just sang."

She wanted to write it down in order not to forget it, so she left the washing of the clothes and went to the piano in the sitting room. She found a key that was just right, and worked it out on manuscript paper. She then asked, "Lord, is that okay? Is it all right like that?" The Lord seemed to answer affirmatively, so she went back to the family washing. She said, "It was just that simple." She sincerely felt that she was led of the Holy Spirit that day in the writing of her worship song.

Soon thereafter it was sung in her church, New Life Church in Palmerston North. Visitors from other parts of New Zealand who attended the service took the song back to their churches. Missionaries began to carry it overseas, where it quickly became a favorite. Soon it was being sung in several nations.

"I've had all sorts of people write to me, asking that I add three more verses," Naida says. "But if the Lord had wanted three more verses, He would have given them to me. All that needed to be said was said. The Spirit impressed upon me that it was to be sung as a love song. You are supposed to sing it softly, slowly and reverently, as if He were our lover. This is what He wanted."

MORE PRECIOUS THAN SILVER

Words and Music by Lynn DeShazo

In 1978, after graduating from Auburn University with a degree in Recreation Administration, Lynn DeShazo took a job at McDonald's. That was not the most likely place for an Auburn alumna to work, but it provided for her livelihood during those first months following graduation. Meanwhile, she was also learning some valuable spiritual lessons as a result of her involvement with Maranatha Ministries, a campus church at Auburn. Lynn was learning that Christians should occasionally fast, and that fasting was a Scriptural method of spiritual growth.

One Wednesday the manager at McDonald's assigned her to "fry duty," the task of cooking the French fries. Unfortunately, it happened to be a day of fasting for her. Needless to say, the battle was on! The fries smelled oh, so good! As the day wore on, her hunger made the idea of breaking of her fast by eating just a couple of those delicious French fries seem insignificant. So, after looking around to make sure that no one would see her, she slipped a few fries into her mouth. At that moment she was almost overcome with guilt—guilt that was twofold: she had broken her fast, and she had done it with stolen French fries.

At the end of her work day, she hurriedly went to a place where she could be alone and deal with the mental and spiritual anguish she felt as a result of this incident. She earnestly asked the Lord's forgiveness for breaking her fast, and for taking something that did not belong to her. She found answers in the Bible—Colossians chapter 2, particularly verse 7, where she read that in Christ are the hidden "treasures of wisdom and knowledge." She also read Proverbs chapter 8, which reveals that spiritual things are more valuable than silver, gold or precious jewels, and that the earthly things we desire cannot be compared to them.

Lynn began to play her guitar, and the Lord poured a new song into her heart. All of a sudden, there it was—"More Precious Than Silver." At that moment she felt so blessed. Just as the guilt had been twofold, so was the blessing. She was freed from the feelings of guilt, and she had a brand-new worship song.

She shared the song with Mark Vosel, the worship leader of the campus church. He thought it was great, and used it in subsequent worship services. He also encouraged Lynn to continue in her songwriting. "More Precious Than Silver" was published by Integrity Music in 1982. It has since been translated into several languages and continues to be sung around the world.

SHOUT TO THE LORD

Words and Music by Darlene Zschech.

Darlene Zschech is known around the world as a singer, songwriter, worship leader and speaker, most notably for spearheading the music that comes from Hillsong Church in her native Australia. According to Darlene, the writing of "Shout to the Lord" was no big occasion. All of the attention that the song received has caused Darlene to be humbled before the Lord and thank Him for His gifts and goodness. When she wrote this song, she didn't think of herself as a songwriter at all.

During a time when she was experiencing some dark days, Darlene sat down at an old piano and began to improvise. A song began to flow from her heart. It was inspired by Psalm 96, a Scripture that she had just read. She continued to sing the song again and again. Suddenly she realized that her depression had lifted, and that her faith and joy in the Lord had returned. The Psalm had focused her mind completely on the Heavenly Father.

Darlene thought to herself, "I think the Lord has given me a worship song." She reluctantly mentioned it to Geoff Bullock, a music pastor at the church, and to Russell Fragar, telling them that she had written what she thought to be a worship song. They asked her to play and sing it for them. With many apologies, and despite a fit of nervousness, she agreed to do so. She became so fearful and shy about the whole situation that she asked Bullock and Fragar to turn and face the wall, looking away from her. Her hands were so sweaty and shaky that it was difficult for her to play the piano. After she finished singing the song, they turned around and told her how magnificent it was. She thought they were just being polite.

After being sung at Hillsong Church, "Shout to the Lord" quickly spread to thousands of churches in many nations around the world. A testimony of the wide acceptance of this song came in April 2008, when it was used on "American Idol," the nation's highest-rated television show.

THERE IS NONE LIKE YOU

Words and Music by Lenny LeBlanc

As a teenager, Lenny LeBlanc bought a guitar with money he made by working at Eckerds. He taught himself to play, and by age 17 he was supporting himself financially with his music. He went on to a very successful career in pop music, as a studio musician on recordings for singers such as Crystal Gayle, Joan Baez, Roy Orbison, Hank Williams, Jr., and The Supremes, to name a few.

Lenny said, "One day a friend sent me a Bible, and for the next few weeks God began to reveal His love to me. I began to realize how shallow and selfish my life was, and there in my home I cried out to Jesus for mercy and forgiveness. I could have continued in the field of pop music, but I sensed that God had something different for me."

One morning while at home alone, Lenny was playing his keyboard when suddenly a tune and some lyrics began coming to him. Soon he had written the major part of a song which he titled "There Is None Like You." He began to weep because of the overwhelming feeling of the goodness of the Lord. He said, "I found it hard to believe that God would give me such a wonderful song. Because it was so meaningful to me I soon had it committed to memory."

A few months later, Lenny's song was launched and would find its way around the world on the wings of an Integrity Music project called *Pure Heart*. The album was recorded live at Faith Tabernacle in Florence, Alabama. The song was performed as a "duet" by Lenny LeBlanc and Kelly Willard—her vocal part was pre-recorded, while Lenny sang his part live.

Several years ago, Lenny accompanied Don Moen on a trip to Korea, where they were engaged in some extraordinary meetings in an outdoor square with 60,000 young people present. During one of the sessions they sang "There Is None Like You" in English. Don then asked the audience to sing it in their own language. Much to Lenny's surprise, they already knew it. The song had been translated into Korean some time before. Someone said to him, "Didn't you know that your song is one of the most popular Christian songs, if not the most popular, throughout all of Asia?" He was completely overwhelmed. The song has been translated into at least six Asian languages.

WE FALL DOWN

Words and Music by Chris Tomlin

Chris Tomlin has written some 200 songs, and approximately 40 of them have been recorded or published. Following is an account of how he wrote "We Fall Down."

Louie Giglio was speaking at a youth conference and Chris Tomlin was one of the worship leaders. Chris had only recently met Louie. At this particular conference, Louie was teaching on Revelation chapter 4, which pictures the throne room of God with the angels and the living creatures around the throne. The twenty-four elders fall down before Him and say, "Thou art worthy, O Lord, to receive glory and honor and power..." Chris said, "I was really taken by the teaching. Our worship should be a response to God when He has revealed something to us. I felt that I had just seen a bit of the picture of the throne room of God."

Later that night in his hotel room, Chris took his guitar and, with his Bible open to Revelation chapter 4, he began to sing, "We fall down, we lay our crowns at the feet of Jesus." He said, "I had no idea where the melody was coming from. I was blown away by the experience."

Chris went to Louie's room and knocked on the door. When Louie opened the door, Chris said, "Tonight you spoke on Revelation chapter 4, and I have just written a song based on that Scripture passage. May I sing it for you?" He politely listened as Chris sang. When he had finished the song, Louie just stared at him. That was not at all the response Chris was hoping for. Then Louie said, "I think the whole world is going to sing that song." The statement surprised Chris and he said, "I don't know about the whole world singing it—I was just wondering if we could sing it tomorrow night."

About six months later, Chris was attending a Christian conference in Austin, Texas, with about 2,000 people present. He suddenly heard a familiar melody being played on the piano. It was "We Fall Down." Sam Perry, the worship leader, sang it and then led the congregation of young people as they sang it. Chris had never heard anyone lead one of his songs. "We Fall Down" has since been translated into many languages and is sung around the world.

BLESSED BE YOUR NAME

Words and Music by MATT REDMAN
and BETH REDMAN

*Recorded a half step lower.

FIRM FOUNDATION

Words and Music by NANCY GORDON
and JAMIE HARVILL

DAYS OF ELIJAH

Words and Music by
ROBIN MARK

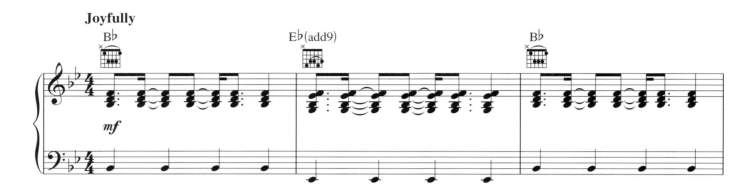

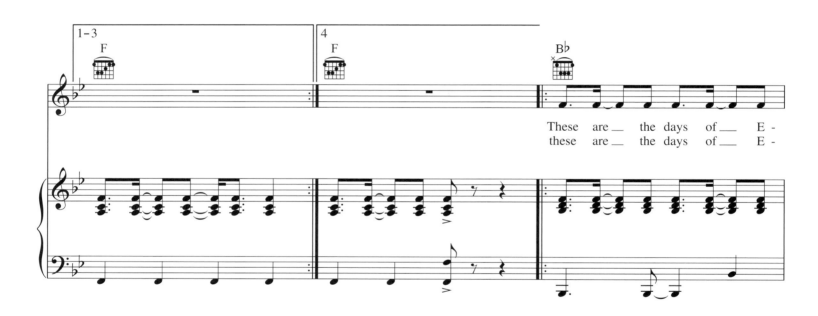

These are __ the days of __ E-
these are __ the days of __ E-

li - jah, __ de - clar - ing __ the Word of __ the Lord. And
ze - kiel, __ the dry bones __ be - com - ing __ as flesh. And

CELEBRATE JESUS

Words and Music by
GARY OLIVER

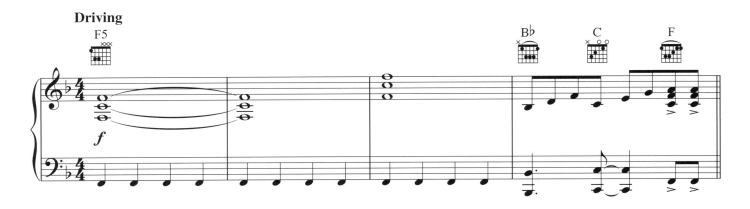

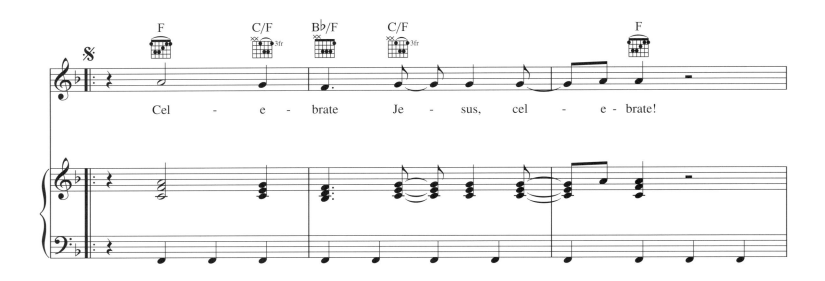

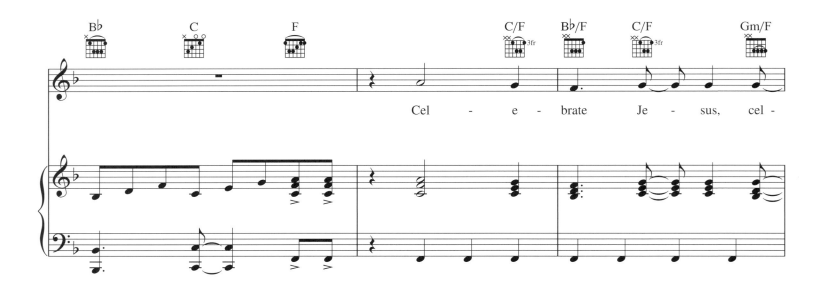

GIVE THANKS

Words and Music by
HENRY SMITH

FOREVER

Words and Music by
CHRIS TOMLIN

GOD OF WONDERS

Words and Music by MARC BYRD
and STEVE HINDALONG

GOD WILL MAKE A WAY

Words and Music by
DON MOEN

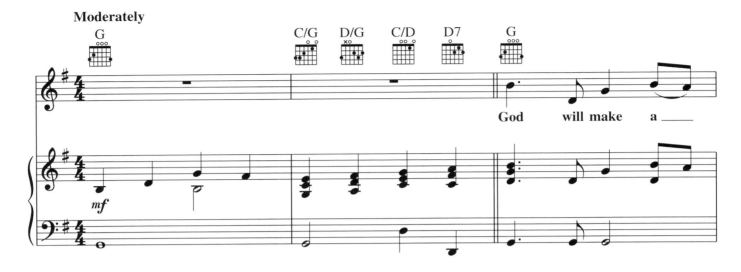

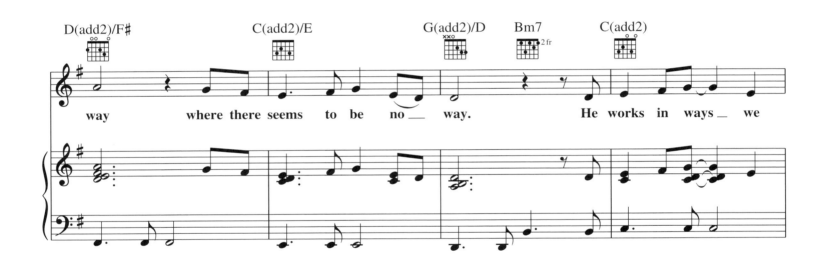

GREAT IS THE LORD

Words and Music by MICHAEL W. SMITH
and DEBORAH D. SMITH

HE IS EXALTED

Words and Music by
TWILA PARIS

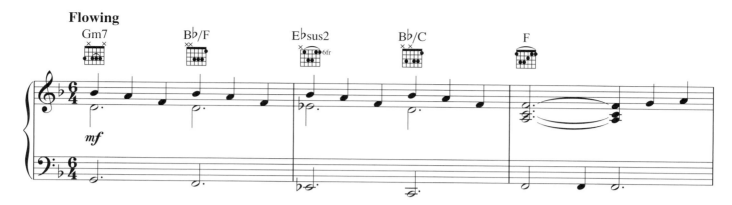

THE HEART OF WORSHIP

Words and Music by
MATT REDMAN

JESUS, NAME ABOVE ALL NAMES

Words and Music by
NAIDA HEARN

HOLY IS THE LORD

Words and Music by CHRIS TOMLIN
and LOUIE GIGLIO

I SING PRAISES

Words and Music by
TERRY MacALMON

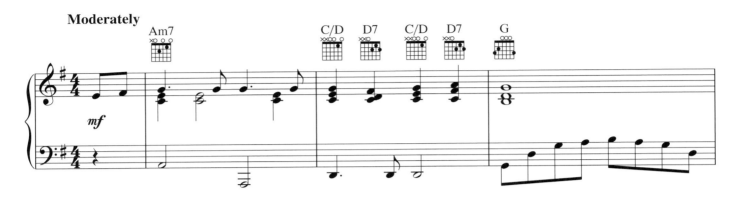

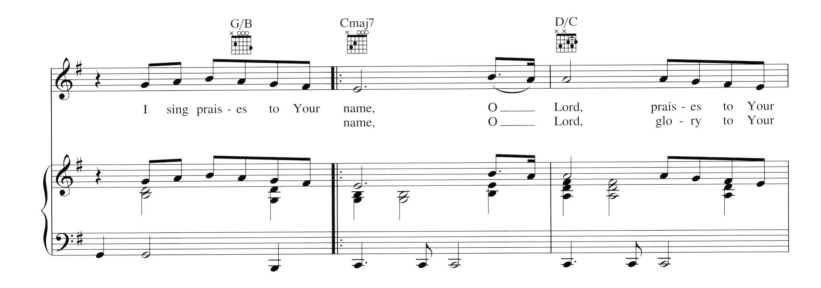

I sing prais-es to Your name, O _____ Lord, prais-es to Your
name, O _____ Lord, glo-ry to Your

name, O _____ Lord, for Your name is great and
name, O _____ Lord, for Your name is great and

I STAND IN AWE

Words and Music by
MARK ALTROGGE

I WORSHIP YOU, ALMIGHTY GOD

Words and Music by
SONDRA CORBETT-WOOD

MORE PRECIOUS THAN SILVER

Words and Music by
LYNN DeSHAZO

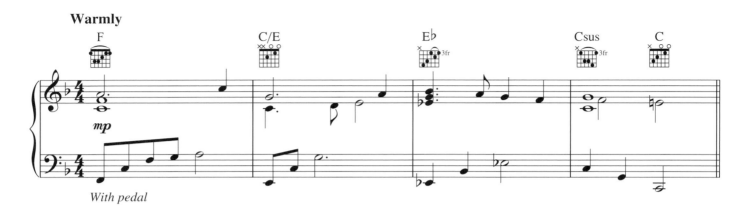

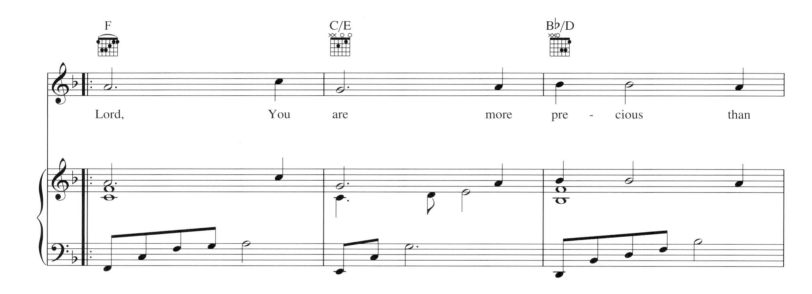

SHOUT TO THE LORD

Words and Music by
DARLENE ZSCHECH

THERE IS NONE LIKE YOU

Words and Music by
LENNY LeBLANC

Worshipfully

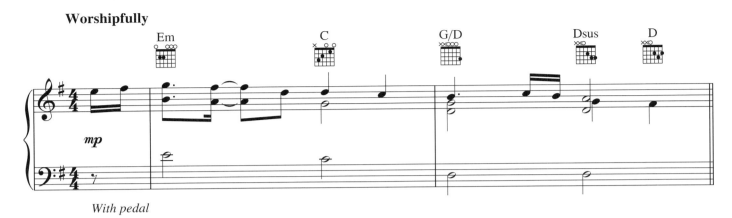

mp

With pedal

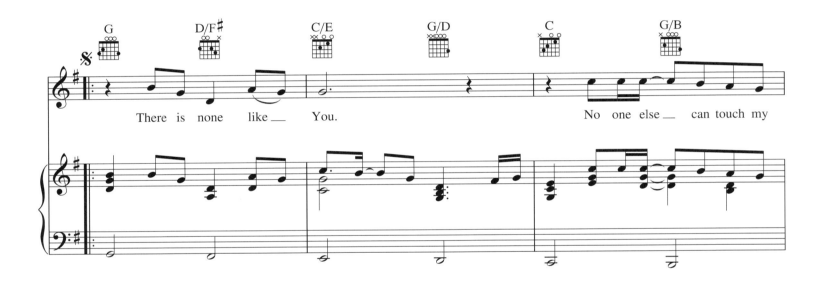

There is none like ___ You. No one else ___ can touch my

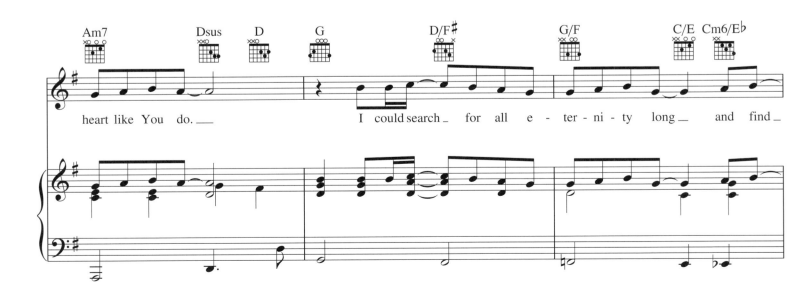

heart like You do. ___ I could search ___ for all e - ter - ni - ty long ___ and find ___

WE FALL DOWN

Words and Music by
CHRIS TOMLIN

Worshipfully

We fall __ down, __ we lay our __ crowns __ at the feet __ of Je-

-sus, _____ the great-ness __ of __ mer-cy and __ love __ at the feet

__ of Je- sus. And we cry, "Ho- ly, ho- ly, ho-

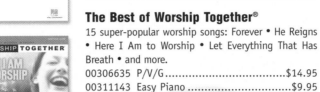

The Best Praise & Worship
Songbooks for Piano

Above All
THE PHILLIP KEVEREN SERIES
15 beautiful praise song piano solo arrangements, perfect for home or congregational use. Includes: Agnus Dei • Ancient of Days • Breathe • Draw Me Close • I Stand in Awe • I Want to Know You • More Love, More Power • Step by Step • We Fall Down • more.
00311024 Piano Solo $11.95

The Best of Worship Together®
15 super-popular worship songs: Forever • He Reigns • Here I Am to Worship • Let Everything That Has Breath • and more.
00306635 P/V/G $14.95
00311143 Easy Piano $9.95

The Best Praise & Worship Songs Ever
80 all-time favorites: Breathe • Days of Elijah • Here I Am to Worship • I Could Sing of Your Love Forever • Open the Eyes of My Heart • Shout to the Lord • We Bow Down • dozens more.
00311057 P/V/G $19.95

The Best Praise & Worship Songs Ever – Easy Piano
Over 70 of the best P&W songs today, including: Awesome God • Blessed Be Your Name • Days of Elijah • Here I Am to Worship • Open the Eyes of My Heart • Shout to the Lord • We Fall Down • and more.
00311312 Easy Piano $19.95

Here I Am to Worship
30 top songs from such CCM stars as Rebecca St. James, Matt Redman, and others. Includes: Be Glorified • Enough • It Is You • Let My Words Be Few • Majesty • We Fall Down • You Alone • more.
00313270 P/V/G $14.95

Here I Am to Worship – For Kids
This great songbook lets the kids join in on 20 of the best modern worship songs, including: God of Wonders • He Is Exalted • The Heart of Worship • Song of Love • Wonderful Maker • and more.
00316098 Easy Piano $14.95

I Could Sing of Your Love Forever
THE PHILLIP KEVEREN SERIES
15 worship songs arranged for solo piano: Holy Ground • I Could Sing of Your Love Forever • I Love You Lord • In This Very Room • My Utmost for His Highest • The Potter's Hand • The Power of Your Love • Shout to the North • more.
00310905 Piano Solo $12.95

Modern Worship
THE CHRISTIAN MUSICIAN SERIES
35 favorites of contemporary congregations, including: All Things Are Possible • Ancient of Days • The Heart of Worship • Holiness • I Could Sing of Your Love Forever • I Will Exalt Your Name • It Is You • We Fall Down • You Are My King (Amazing Love) • and more.
00310957 P/V/G $14.95

Shout to the Lord!
THE PHILLIP KEVEREN SERIES
Moving arrangements of 14 praise song favorites, including: As the Deer • Great Is the Lord • More Precious than Silver • Oh Lord, You're Beautiful • Shine, Jesus, Shine • Shout to the Lord • Thy Word • and more.
00310699 Piano Solo $12.95

Timeless Praise
THE PHILLIP KEVEREN SERIES
20 songs of worship arranged for easy piano by Phillip Keveren: El Shaddai • Give Thanks • How Beautiful • How Majestic Is Your Name • Oh Lord, You're Beautiful • People Need the Lord • Seek Ye First • There Is a Redeemer • Thy Word • and more.
00310712 Easy Piano $12.95

Worship Together® Favorites
All Over the World • Cry Out to Jesus • Empty Me • Everlasting God • Forever • Happy Day • Holy Is the Lord • How Deep the Father's Love for Us • How Great Is Our God • Indescribable • Join the Song • Ready for You • Wholly Yours • Yes You Have • You Never Let Go.
00313360 P/V/G $16.95

Worship Together® Favorites for Kids
Enough • Everlasting God • Forever • From the Inside Out • Holy Is the Lord • How Great Is Our God • Made to Worship • Mountain of God • Wholly Yours • The Wonderful Cross • Yes You Have • You Never Let Go.
00316109 Easy Piano $12.95

Worship Together® Platinum
22 of the best contemporary praise & worship songs: Be Glorified • Better Is One Day • Draw Me Close • Every Move I Make • Here I Am to Worship • I Could Sing of Your Love Forever • O Praise Him (All This for a King) • and more.
00306721 P/V/G $16.95

Worship – The Ultimate Collection
Matching folio with 24 top worship favorites, including: God of Wonders • He Reigns • Hungry (Falling on My Knees) • Lord, Reign in Me • Open the Eyes of My Heart • Yesterday, Today and Forever • and more.
00313337 P/V/G $17.95

FOR MORE INFORMATION, SEE YOUR LOCAL MUSIC DEALER, OR WRITE TO:

HAL•LEONARD® CORPORATION
7777 W. BLUEMOUND RD. P.O. BOX 13819 MILWAUKEE, WI 53213

For complete song lists and to view our entire catalog of titles, please visit www.halleonard.com

Prices, contents, and availability subject to change without notice.

0408